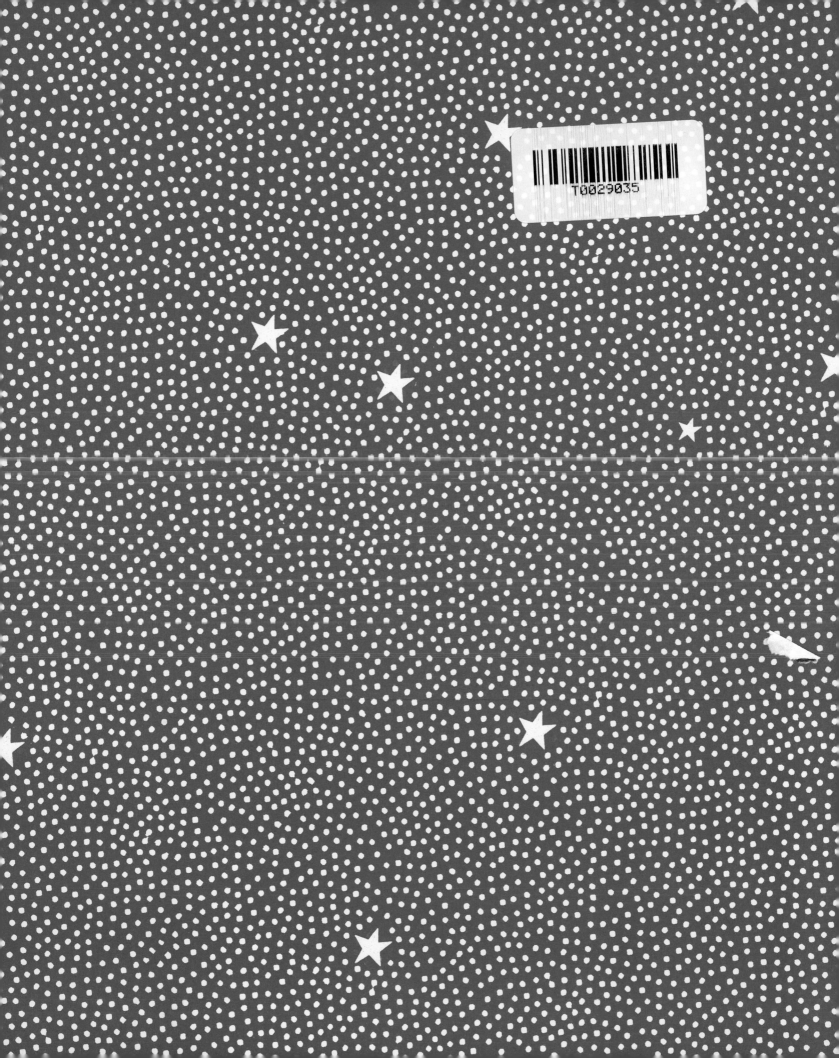

THE MIND-BLOWING
WORLD OF EXTRAORDINARY
COMPETITIONS

MEET THE INCREDIBLE PEOPLE WHO
WILL COMPETE AT *ANYTHING*

NEON SQUID

Contents

Introduction

Humans love to compete with one another. We're not the only species that does it—lots of male animals fight it out to see who has the biggest antlers or horns, or the strongest muscles. Male birds-of-paradise hold elaborate dance-offs with one another, hoping to impress any females who might be watching. But no other animal on the planet has achieved our sheer variety of contests, with all kinds of complicated rules and rewards for winning.

Birds-of-paradise hold dance competitions.

Contests aren't a newfangled thing—far from it! In the earliest days of human evolution, our ancestors competed with other animals (and among themselves) for food, shelter, and safety. We've been wild about contests for thousands of years, from wrestling in ancient Greece to tug-of-war in ancient Egypt, ball games in Aztec and Maya cities, and poetry battles among the Vikings. The game of chess is thought to have originated in India around 1,500 years ago, while 2,000 years ago in China, rival villages raced each other in dragon boats. People all over the world love to test their skills for fame and riches, or just for the glory of winning and bragging rights!

Ancient Egyptian tug-of-war

This book is full of the wild, creative, and amazing ways that people compete with one another. Come along for a tour of some of the most incredible, most unusual, and silliest competitions from all over the world and throughout history. Learn about early Chinese donkey polo and the ancient Celtic strength competitions that have become today's Highland Games. Do you have a competitive spirit? One of the contests in this book might mean there's a future trophy with your name on it! Become a champion vegetable grower, and raise cabbages the size of beach balls. Train your pet bunny to be a champion show jumper, or play the most incredible riffs on your air guitar. The possibilities are endless!

ANNA GOLDFIELD

Don't try this at home!

Some of the competitions in this book can be dangerous. Do not try these at home. The people who compete at them are trained experts. You can try growing giant vegetables though!

Dragon boat racing is part of an ancient Chinese festival that began over 2,500 years ago. Teams of racers sit in a single row in a long, sleek boat that is decorated to look like the body of a Chinese dragon. Often, the prows of the boats are adorned with fiercely snarling dragon heads. Competitors have to summon the spirit of a dragon to win the race!

PADDLE TO THE BEAT

During a race, competitors paddle to the rhythm of the drummer seated at the front of the boat. That rhythm is seen as the "heart of the dragon." Today dragon boat racing is a competitive sport across China, with thousands of participants every year. Some believe dragon boat racing began as a worship ceremony to Qu Yuan, a poet from the Warring States Period (475–221 BCE) who drowned on the Miluo River in southern China. Others believe that the first participants in dragon boat racing were superstitious villagers who celebrated the fifth day of the fifth lunar month of the Chinese calendar (believed to be an unlucky day) by worshipping a mystical dragon. Villagers would hold a ceremony and make offerings to the dragon, then the race was on!

Dragon Boat Racing

A RACE TO WARD OFF MISFORTUNE

PROTECTION FROM EVIL

According to historical accounts, villagers believed keeping the dragon happy would free them from misfortune and encourage rains needed for farming. Dragon boat racing was also a way they believed they could protect themselves against the evils of the fifth lunar month, when poisonous animals would come out of their winter hiding places.

LUNAR CALENDAR

The exact date of the dragon boat races is slightly different each year because it is calculated using the lunar calendar, which is based on the movements of the moon. This reflects a period when farmers used the phases of the moon to plan when various crops would be planted.

The Jumping Frog Jubilee

HOW FAR DO *YOU* THINK YOU COULD GO IN THREE BIG JUMPS?

Since 1928, people and their frogs have been hopping down to Calaveras County, California, to compete in the Jumping Frog Jubilee. The skilled "frog jockeys" urge their frogs to jump record-breaking distances using special techniques. But don't worry—these jockeys don't actually ride the frogs!

AMAZING AMPHIBIANS

Strategies in this contest include shouting encouragement to the frog, jumping behind the frog to startle it forward, or blowing a puff of air at the frog's behind. Each frog in the competition is allowed three jumps in a row, and the distance of those jumps is combined to make the total score. The American bullfrog is the species usually entered in the contest—it is illegal to use any species that aren't naturally from the area. Usually, the really dedicated frog jockeys bring their own locally caught frogs with them. But if you're a more casual competitor, you can rent a frog at the Jubilee!

Record

The current world record for a frog jump at this competition is 21 ft 5¾ in (655 cm), set in 1986 by a frog named Rosie the Ribiter. There is a $5,000 prize for beating this record, but to date no one has claimed it.

A group of frogs is called an army.

CALM COMPETITORS

The frogs are pampered during the competition. The number of jumps they can take per day is limited, so no frog gets too tired. Calming music plays in their enclosures when they're not competing.

MARK TWAIN

Frog-jumping was inspired by a short story written by the famous author Mark Twain (who wrote *The Adventures of Huckleberry Finn*). The short story was originally published in 1865 with the title *Jim Smiley and His Jumping Frog*. It was later changed to *The Celebrated Jumping Frog of Calaveras County.*

West African Wrestling

FIGHTING IS ONLY THE HALF OF IT

The national sport of Senegal, a country in West Africa, is a type of wrestling called *laamb*. This style of wrestling was recorded as early as the 14th century—more than 600 years ago! Wrestling was a way for young men to stay fit (and out of trouble), and possibly even to attract a marriage partner through an impressive display of their strength.

THE AIM OF THE GAME

The wrestling arena is typically outside, on a sandy surface. Often rituals are performed at the beginning of the matches to make sure that no bad luck affects the wrestlers. The basic goal of a *laamb* match is for each wrestler to try to overpower an opponent and flip them over onto their back, or to force them onto their hands and knees. Some matches allow the use of hands for jabs and punches, while others only allow grappling.

Laamb is a hugely popular professional sport in Senegal, and pros spend months training before their matches. Spiritual preparation is a major part of the training process.

A TOAST TO THE BOASTS

A major part of a *laamb* match isn't physical at all—it's a boasting contest called *bàkk*. This is a performance of storytelling, poems, or songs in which a wrestler brags about their accomplishments and their skill at wrestling. By doing this they hope to strike fear into the heart of their opponent. It adds artistic elegance to the show of physical strength. To truly excel at this type of wrestling, you've got to have brains and brawn!

Wrestlers often wear protective charms or amulets called gris-gris (pronounced "gree-gree") to give them luck in the arena.

The Battle of the Oranges

THINGS ARE ABOUT TO GET JUICY

Each year in the town of Ivrea in Northwest Italy, teams of townspeople dressed in "armor" throw oranges at each other! This citrus fight is a recreation of a 12th century battle, when the town's inhabitants revolted against the harsh rule of a tyrannical duke.

AN EPIC BATTLE

The battle lasts for three days. Each team of orange-throwers, or *aranceri*, has a separate location in the city. Some participants hurl oranges while running through the city on foot. Other team members throw fruit from moving carts. Local shop fronts (and spectators) are protected from any stray projectiles with nets. During the event, more than 700 tons of oranges are thrown and crushed underfoot! Afterward, the mess is cleared up and the crushed fruit is brought to a food waste center.

DON'T MESS WITH VIOLETTA

According to legend, the duke tried to force his romantic attentions on a local miller's daughter, Violetta. He got more than he bargained for, though, when Violetta grabbed a sword and chopped off his head! The townspeople, fed up with the duke and his soldiers, stormed the duke's castle and burned it to the ground.

Although it's a mock battle, people have been injured by flying oranges. Going to Ivrea at festival time? Pack a helmet!

CHOOSE YOUR WEAPON

Oranges have been used in this battle as ammunition since the late 1800s. Before that, however, the battle was fought with whatever extra food was handy—including apples, and even beans!

ORANGES FROM THE SOUTH

Today, the oranges that are used for the battle are rejects from the Sicilian winter harvest and would otherwise be discarded. They're shipped north from Sicily to Ivrea for the festival.

Ivrea

Sicily

Chessboxing

A BATTLE OF BRAINS AND FISTS

What happens when you combine chess with boxing? You get chessboxing! And yes, it's exactly what it sounds like. You might think that chess and boxing have very little in common, but both require a lot of strategy. Competitors must be able to think on their feet and concentrate hard, planning their next chess moves while dodging an opponent's swinging fists.

ONE BATTLE, TWO BATTLEFIELDS

The rules of chessboxing are pretty simple, as long as you know how to play chess and how to box! A full game lasts 11 rounds, with players alternating between three-minute boxing bouts and four-minute chess sessions.

WHO WINS?

Between boxing rounds and chess rounds, players get a little extra time to take off their boxing gloves. It would be tricky to hold the chess pieces otherwise! A player only wins if they reach checkmate in the chess game or a knockout in the boxing ring—whichever comes first. What other sports and games would you like to try combining? Rugby darts? Karate cards? Hockey hangman? Mix and match your favorites at home!

The sport was invented in 1992 by a French comic book artist named Enki Bilal.

Dodge

The more punches the pros avoid, the better their chess moves tend to be!

ANCIENT GAMES

Boxing and chess both have ancient origins. The earliest archaeological evidence for fist-fighting comes from western Asia in the 2nd and 3rd century BCE—more than 2,200 years ago! The oldest known chess pieces (carved from ivory taken from elephants) were excavated in what is today Samarkand, Uzbekistan, and date to around 760 CE.

32, 33, 34...

Sheep's wool reflects ultraviolet rays from the sun, protecting sheep from sunburn.

Sheep Counting

IT'S NOT JUST FOR FALLING ASLEEP!

Raising sheep for their meat, wool, and milk is a big deal in Australia, so there are plenty of sheep farmers, and even more sheep! The very first National Sheep Counting Championships were held in 2002 in the state of New South Wales. The rules are very simple: a group of sheep run at top speed past a group of competitors, who do their best to count them all as they zoom by. At the first competition, the winner correctly counted 277 sheep.

6, 7, 8...

SHEEP SHIPS

Sheep aren't originally from Australia. They were brought over in the 1700s with shiploads of colonists arriving from Europe. Counting sheep is a daily part of sheep farming, and while automated cameras and drones now perform some of the work, a farmer might still count thousands of sheep a day!

ANCIENT LIVESTOCK

Sheep were first tamed by humans sometime around 11,000 BCE in Mesopotamia, a region in the Middle East. Wild sheep naturally shed their winter wool in the spring, but modern domesticated sheep don't. Instead, they have to be sheared by farmers.

In 2021, a sheep named Baarack that had escaped from a farm in Australia was found. No one knows how long he was on the run, but he'd grown more than 77 lb (35 kg) of wool!

Building Big Things

Humans build giant models of things for all sorts of reasons. It might be to create a novelty attraction, to show off some engineering skills, or to try to outdo one another. It's also a creative way to advertise a business, or to just have some fun! It's funny to see a giant version of something that is usually very small, like an ant or an apple.

DOWN UNDER CREATIONS

Australia is the place to go for giant models of things. There are around 150 novelty objects dotted around the country! They include the Giant Mushroom, the Big Golden Guitar, the Big Poo (!), Matilda the Kangaroo, the Big Prawn, and Larry the Big Lobster.

BIG BOAR

Woinic, the world's largest boar, is a tourist attraction located in northern France. This big fellow is built from steel sheets and has a trapdoor in his belly. Woinic was built by sculptor Eric Sléziak, who took ten years to finish his creation. The boar stands on a rotating platform, so visitors can admire him from all angles.

THE KING OF STRING

There are, if you can believe it, multiple claims for the world's largest ball of string. The largest ball of twine made by a single person is the work of American James Frank Kotera, who started winding in 1979. The largest ball of string created by a community is in Cawker City, Kansas. This monster is being added to all the time. If you ever need some spare string, you know where to go!

ROCK ON!

Casey, a city in Illinois, has a population of just over 2,000 people. Nevertheless, it's home to around a dozen oversized objects, including a rocking chair, a working seesaw, and a giant mailbox – from which you can actually send letters!

People have lived in **Australia** for more than **65,000 years!** There's no record of the first Australians to build giant lobsters or mushrooms, though.

A contest held in Shaoyang, China, tests beekeepers' bravery by seeing how many bees a single person can attract to their body with a single queen bee. Contestants stand on a scale and use nose plugs so bees don't wander into their nostrils. After one hour, judges weigh the bees on each contestant and declare a winner!

ORIGINS

In the 1830s, a Ukrainian beekeeper named Petro Prokopovych was the first ever person to model a beard formed from hundreds of bees. He did this by keeping a queen bee in a tiny cage under his chin. The male worker bees, who like to stay close to their queen, landed on his face, forming a magnificent, buzzing beard!

WHAT IS BEARDING?

"Bearding" is actually a natural activity performed by bees. It refers to clusters of bees hanging out on a hive in a beard-like shape. They do this to make room inside the hive for good air flow (ventilation) and to keep the hive cool on hot days to protect their larvae (baby bees).

Bee–Bearding

WOULD YOU LET BEES HANG OUT ON YOUR FACE?

In 2018, a man set the record for bee–bearding by holding 60,000 bees on his face.

FOLLOW THE GUIDE

As well as wearing bees, humans like to eat their honey! The honey guide bird uses a special call to tell people that there are beehives nearby. While the humans use smoke to calm the bees and harvest honey from a tree, the bird helps itself to the bee larvae.

Tip

Got a bee on you? Hold still so you don't get stung! It will leave when it realizes you're not a flower.

Competitors are challenged with different fabrics and a whole range of environments.

Extreme Ironing

THIS SPORT IS ANYTHING BUT A CHORE!

Participants in extreme ironing combine the thrills of extreme sports in dangerous locations with the satisfaction of a nicely pressed garment. In 1980, a man named Tony Hiam noticed that his brother-in-law always ironed his shirts, even when camping in a tent. As a little joke, Tony started bringing an ironing board to various odd locations to take pictures of himself ironing, and to cause passersby to do a double take. What would you do if you saw someone ironing their shirt up in the branches of a tree?

Extreme ironing has taken place on a surfboard in the ocean, on a specially built rock climbing wall, and even on a unicycle!

SMOOTH PERFORMANCES

Tony's joke has since expanded to performances of extreme ironing by people in *lots* of different places! These have included mountainsides mid-climb, on top of large bronze statues, in the middle of a busy highway, in forests, in a canoe, mid-skydive, and even under the ice of a frozen lake. Ironing in the middle of a lake seems like a questionable way to wind up with a crisp shirt, but it makes a great story!

IRONING INVENTIONS

The first portable ironing board was created by an inventor named Sarah Boone in 1892. The board's shape made it easier to iron the sleeves and bodies of ladies' dresses. Sarah was one of the first Black women to be issued a patent (so others couldn't claim it as their own invention) in the United States.

Camel Beauty Pageants

WHAT LOVELY EYELASHES YOU HAVE!

What's the most beautiful animal in the world? Did you say camel? If so, this is the competition for you. In the United Arab Emirates, a country in the Middle East, there are annual camel beauty contests held to celebrate Bedouin tribal culture. The Bedouin are a group of nomadic tribes that have historically lived in the desert regions of the Arabian Peninsula, North Africa, and Western Asia. Traditionally, the Bedouin livelihood was made by herding animals such as sheep, goats, and—of course—camels.

STRIKE A POSE

Camels were first domesticated by humans in the Arabian Peninsula around 3,000 years ago. They have been important as sources of meat, milk, and woven fabrics since then. It's unclear when exactly the first camel beauty contest was held, though some believe it can be traced to a feud between two families in 1993. They were fighting over whose camels were lovelier and called on independent judges to decide the winner!

IDEAL CAMEL

What exactly makes a camel beautiful? The competition is divided into different categories, depending on who owns the camels, but the judges are always looking for the same things.

The lips have to be perfectly soft and droopy.

The camel's neck must be long and elegant, with the right curve.

The ideal camel has to have long, straight legs.

CAMEL COUSINS

There were once wild camels living across North America, but they were wiped out around 10,000 years ago. This was after the first people began to travel to the Americas, so the North American camel population may have been affected by hunting. You won't find any wild camels in the Americas anymore, but in South America, you might find their close cousins: llamas and alpacas!

The camel has to have perky ears, which are sometimes decorated with earrings.

The hump must be shapely and positioned on the camel's lower back.

The eyes have to be soulful, with long, curling eyelashes.

Posture is key; you don't want your camel to slouch!

The camel's coat has to be sleek, shiny, and soft.

23

Do-Nothing Contest

IT'S HARDER THAN IT SOUNDS...

On one day each year, in several towns in South Korea, doing nothing is a competitive sport. The goal is to zone out without losing focus—to keep your mind as blank as possible and your heartbeat steady. Contestants have to control their breathing, keeping it slow and steady. At the end of 90 minutes, the contestant with the slowest heart rate wins—though falling asleep automatically results in disqualification!

THE EXPERTS

There are plenty of animals who thrive on not doing much, though they might be disqualified from a do-nothing contest. Sloths, koalas, pythons, hippos, and opossums all sleep between 10 and 20 hours per day!

A SENSE OF CALM

The contest was started as a way to contrast the Zen calm of doing nothing, in a serene place like a forest, with the busy daily lives of people living in cities. Zen is a branch of Buddhism and focuses on understanding the true nature of both the world and one's own self. Self-control and discipline are also an important part of Zen philosophy. In the modern world, when people work hard, they often reward themselves with delicious food and drink, or by purchasing an item they've had their eye on. The do-nothing contest (also known as the "space out" contest) is a way to reward hard work with some time dedicated to relaxation, while also practicing Zen principles.

THE RULES

It sounds simple, but doing nothing means no phones, talking, laughing, sleeping, texting, or going to the bathroom! Science has shown that our brains need downtime to process new knowledge and memories. So, sometimes doing nothing is good for you!

Amazing Facial Hair

THE FINEST FACIAL FURNITURE IN THE WORLD

Every two years, the World Beard and Moustache Association hosts a competition for people who have grown out their beards and waxed their whiskers into lengthy, luxurious, highly styled creations. There are three brackets in which contestants can enter their exquisitely groomed facial hair: moustache, partial beard, and full beard.

There are many different types of moustache, including the Dalí (named after the surrealist painter Salvador Dalí). Contestants can opt to grow a handlebar moustache, which curls up at the sides, or a walrus-style 'stache, which droops down toward the chin.

Partial beard styles include the musketeer (small, thin moustache and small, pointy beard), the Alaskan whaler (beard without moustache), and the imperial (hair on cheeks and upper lip only).

A HAIRY HISTORY

Beards have had a long and varied history in cultures throughout the world. Ancient Egyptian pharaohs wore false beards made of metal that were tied on with a ribbon. This was a symbol of their high status. In ancient Persia, men groomed their beards with scented oils. The wealthier you were, the fancier your beard! Alexander the Great, the Macedonian conqueror, ordered his soldiers to shave their beards so they couldn't be grabbed by enemy soldiers in battle.

LONGEST BEARD

The record holder outside of the world competition was a Norwegian-American man named Hans Nilson Langseth, born in 1846 (he didn't have a beard when he was born, though). His beard was more than 17½ ft (5 m) long! In 1967, the beard was presented to the Smithsonian Museum of Natural History in Washington, D.C.

If you're sporting a long beard, you could style it into a Garibaldi: wide at the bottom but no more than 8 in (20 cm) in length. For a shorter version, try the Verdi: a beard with a curled-up moustache.

MOVE OVER, ARNIE

Katie Sandwina was born in 1884 in Vienna, Austria, and became world-famous for her incredible strongwoman performances. Katie wowed crowds with feats such as bending steel bars and lifting her husband over her head with one hand—while wearing high heels!

Eugen Sandow, a professional bodybuilder, was only able to lift a 300-lb (136-kg) barbell up to his chest.

Katie defeated celebrity strongman Eugen by lifting the same weight over her head.

Feats of Strength

Physical strength is a point of pride and competition for many people, today and throughout history. Fitness-based sports are extremely popular throughout the world, and both men and women compete to show off their strength and muscular physiques. The human body can do some incredible things!

CANNONBALL

In the 1870s, a man named John Holtum performed a cannonball catch to prove his strength. An assistant would fire a cannon pointed directly at him, and John would catch the ball as it rocketed his way. He lost a few fingers while trying to perfect this act!

HEY, BIG GUY

Angus MacAskill was a Scottish-Canadian man who stood 7 ft 9 in (2.4 m) tall and would often show off his strength by lifting a ship's anchor to chest height. He was also said to have been able to lift a fully grown horse over a fence.

THE HIGHLAND GAMES

The Highland Games have been a part of Scottish history for almost 1,000 years—since the 11th century. Local clan chiefs would hold athletic competitions to determine who were strong and fit enough to be messengers and soldiers for the king. One of these competitions was the lifting of "manhood stones," giant chunks of rock that would be lifted onto nearby walls or ledges as a rite of passage for young men. The modern Highland Games still includes an event where competitors lift a massive concrete ball onto a barrel.

Toe Wrestling

YOU MAY HAVE HEARD OF FEATS OF STRENGTH, BUT WHAT ABOUT STRENGTH OF FEET?

This competition started in a pub in Staffordshire, in the United Kingdom, in 1974. It's very possible that the people who invented toe wrestling had enjoyed a drink or two before coming up with the idea. Champion toe wrestlers take the sport seriously and exercise their toes regularly. It's important to keep the toes and feet in good health before a match, since strained ankles and even broken toes have been known to occur in battle!

TOE-TALLY AWESOME

Smelly socks are not appreciated!

You'll need strong toes to win the World Toe Wrestling Championships. The rules are simple. Players must have bare feet, and each player has to have their feet inspected before entering a match. It is common courtesy within the sport for contestants to remove each other's shoes and socks. Hopefully, everyone competing has recently washed between their toes!

Toe wrestlers sit opposite each other and interlock their big toes. Each contestant then tries to force the other's foot off a platform, using only the strength of their feet and ankles. They compete in three rounds, first with the right foot, then the left, then the right foot again. To progress in the contest you must win at least two out of the three rounds.

The platform is called a toedium.

Olympics?

Fans of the competition applied for entry into the Olympic Games in 1997, but sadly toe wrestling has not yet been made an Olympic sport.

EVOLVING FEET

The shape of the human foot is unique because we evolved to walk and run upright on two legs. Look at the feet of a chimpanzee, our closest living primate relative. In comparison, our toes are very short. Chimp feet look much more like hands, with their big toe positioned like our thumbs are. We have our toes all in a line, which helps us walk. Chimps are great at picking things up with their feet and climbing trees, but they can't walk upright or run nearly as well as we can!

Human

Chimpanzee

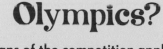

Rabbit Show Jumping

WHO HAS THE TOP HOPS?

Ah, show jumping, where the competitors show off their powerful jumping ability, sleek coats, and... fluffy tails? That's right, this is bunny show jumping. It's modeled after the horse sport of the same name, but rabbits run the course instead.

RUN, RABBIT, RUN!

The sport began in the 1970s in Sweden, where it's called *kaninhoppning*. Today there are contests held all over the world. Bunnies compete on a straight course and a crooked course. On the straight course, the bunnies have to jump obstacles one after the other in a line. On the crooked course, the obstacles are placed on a winding path.

ONE GIANT LEAP FOR RABBITKIND

On the courses, the rabbits are led by their owners, who hold a long leash attached to a harness on their competing bunny. Each rabbit only has two minutes to make it through each course. The rabbit that goes the fastest with the fewest mistakes wins. Rabbits also compete in the high jump and the long jump. The high jump tests the height a rabbit can leap up from the ground, and the long jump tests how far forward the bunny can go in a single bound.

The world record for the highest vertical rabbit jump is just over 3 ft (just under 1 m). It is held by a bunny named Mimrelunds Tösen from Denmark. Domestic rabbits can jump about 10 ft (3 m) horizontally.

On the crooked course, the obstacles *have* to be jumped in the correct order, or the rabbit is disqualified.

Big rabbit

The world's largest rabbit, Darius, is 4¼ ft (1.3 m) long. That's a lot of rabbit!

Areca Nut Tree Climbing

CONTESTANTS SCRAMBLE UP A SLIPPERY TRUNK FOR PRIZES!

Indonesia celebrates its Independence Day on August 17. The day usually includes all sorts of festivals and celebrations throughout the country, but the most unusual of these is *Panjat Pinang*, or climbing the areca nut tree. An areca is a type of palm tree that grows in the tropical areas of the Pacific, Asia, and some parts of eastern Africa. It is also commonly referred to as a betel tree.

Betel seed

CLIMBING THE GREASY POLE

For the climbing contest, a tall, straight areca palm trunk is greased up with oil, and treats and prizes are attached to the top. Audiences cheer on the competitors, rooting for their favorites. Sometimes individual climbers try to reach the top, while other times teammates stand on one another's shoulders to make a human ladder.

Prizes for *Panjat Pinang* include tasty treats, money, and even larger items such as bicycles! Sometimes the prizes are wrapped to keep them a surprise.

Teams have one attempt to reach the top and pull down a prize. After the contest, the whole village often celebrates with a big feast.

DUTCH ORIGINS

This celebration dates to when the Dutch ruled Indonesia as part of their colonial empire. Greased-pole climbing was once a Dutch tradition at parties, and the Dutch brought the tradition to Indonesia. Although Indonesia is now an independent country, the areca nut tree climb is an important part of local tradition.

Peat Bog Snorkeling

A SPORT TO GET REALLY STUCK IN

Usually, people snorkel in crystal clear ocean waters, taking in the beautiful underwater scenery and tropical fish. Not so in Wales, where the World Bog Snorkeling Championships are held. In this sporting event, competitors race through deep, muddy trenches cut into peat bogs. They are not allowed to use their arms. Instead, they must rely on the power of their flapping feet alone!

Competitors must complete two 60-yard (55-m) lengths of a trench cut into the peat.

Speedy

In 2018, champion Neil Rutter managed the course in one minute, eighteen seconds.

BOGGY FUN

Believe it or not, snorkeling isn't the only sport done in bogs! There is a similar event where competitors ride specially modified mountain bikes through bog trenches. The bikes are weighted so they stay underwater, and the riders wear diving weights. They cycle while wearing a snorkel with just their heads poking up above the water.

WHAT IS PEAT?

Peat is formed from layers and layers of decayed grass and leaves falling into a very wet environment and staying waterlogged for many years. Traditionally, these layers were cut into strips and harvested for use as fuel, or to flavor Scottish whisky. However, stored within peat is a lot of the gas carbon dioxide, which is released when it is harvested. This is very bad for the environment, and so today conservationists try to protect peat bogs.

Peat harvester

BOG MUMMIES

Peat bogs are also very interesting to archaeologists. There is almost no oxygen down in those layers of decayed vegetation, so artifacts and even human remains are incredibly well preserved. There are some "bog mummies" that have been excavated from peat bogs in Denmark that are so well preserved that you can still see their hair, clothes, and even the stubble on their chins!

Fat Bear Week

IN THE WORLD OF BEARS, IT'S SURVIVAL OF THE FATTEST

This might be the only contest in this whole book that doesn't involve people at all! At least, not as competitors. Over the course of seven days in late September and early October, park rangers at Katmai National Park in Alaska hold a competition for the local brown bears. Around this time, these large mammals are preparing to go into winter hibernation, and the rangers want to see who is the fattest!

A NICE SPOT FOR FISHING

During hibernation, bears can lose up to a third of their body weight. Cramming themselves full of delicious, fatty salmon from the rivers is key to their survival. The bears snatch the leaping salmon right out of the water! The bears are all tagged and monitored as part of the National Park's efforts to care for the local ecosystem. The public vote online for which bear they think is the fattest, and a winner is crowned—though, for obvious reasons, not literally...

A bear straight out of hibernation...

...and a bear getting ready for hibernation!

Salmon migrate upriver each year to lay their eggs and start a new generation of salmon. Bears and local human populations have relied on these salmon runs for thousands of years.

SLEEPY TIME

Different bear species hibernate for slightly different lengths of time. Brown (grizzly) bears typically spend five to seven months tucked away in dens. During that time, their bodies slow down to preserve energy—but it still means going months without eating or drinking. So when the bears wake up in the spring, the first thing they need to do is eat. Bears can gulp down as many as 40 salmon in a single sitting!

Camel Jumping

TRY NOT TO GET THE HUMP

On the west coast of Yemen, a country in the Middle East, members of the Zaraniq tribe are famous for their local sport: camel jumping. If you're picturing jockeys riding camels over hurdles, think again. In this competition, the camels *are* the hurdles.

Not easy

Competitors need to achieve both height and distance—five camels standing together cover about 15 ft (4.5 m)!

THE RULES ARE SIMPLE

Jumpers compete barefoot and take a long running start, pelting up a short mud ramp before hurling themselves through the air. If any part of a jumper's body touches any of the camels, the jump is disqualified.

PARTY TIME

Each jumper starts by leaping over a single camel. If that jump is successful, another camel is added to the line, and then another, and another. The contestant who is able to clear the highest number of camels is the winner. These contests are typically held at festivals, or at celebrations such as weddings. The best camel jumpers can clear at least five camels!

Crying Baby Festival

SOMETIMES IT PAYS TO BE A CRYBABY

The wrestlers make goofy faces at the babies or gently jiggle them, hoping to make them yell.

The Nakizumo Crying Baby Festival is a Japanese event that has been going on for more than 400 years. Usually, parents don't want a baby to start screaming, but in this case, everyone wants the babies to really let it all out! The origin of the festival traces back to a folk saying that translates to "crying babies grow fat" and was a traditional way to ensure that children had full, healthy lives.

A SOB STORY

These days, the festival honors tradition while also entertaining a crowd. Each year in April, people gather at the Sensō-ji temple in Tokyo to watch babies compete against one another. The babies don't do it alone—each child is paired with a burly sumo wrestler who attempts to make his charge burst into tears by yelling "CRY! CRY!" ("*NAKI NAKI*") into the baby's face.

Pardon?

If you ever get a chance to attend a crying baby festival, you might want to bring some protective earphones.

BABY MILESTONES

It's not just baby-crying; several other Japanese traditions exist to welcome new children.

The seventh night after a baby is born, the parents formally announce the baby's name to the family. Often, the father or mother paints the name and date of birth in Japanese calligraphy.

Around 100 days after a baby is born, families celebrate the ceremony of *okuizome*, or a baby's first "real" meal. Families gather for a large meal and take turns feeding the child bites of food, symbolizing a hope for a prosperous life.

THE WAILERS

The rules of the competition are simple. Two baby-and-sumo-wrestler teams face off at a time. If one of the competing babies cries first, then that baby wins. If both babies wail at the same time, then the one who cries the loudest wins. But don't worry! Each match is short, and afterward, the babies are immediately returned to their parents.

LOUD AND PROUD

Babies can scream at up to 130 decibels. A decibel is a unit used to measure and compare the loudness of sounds, and 130 decibels is about the same volume as a jet engine!

Cheese Rolling

WHAT WOULD YOU RISK FOR CHEESE?

How do you like your cheese? Sliced? Grated? How about rolling away from you down a steep hill? That's the cheese of choice at the Cooper's Hill Cheese Rolling race in Gloucester, England. Traditionally, the race features a large wheel of Double Gloucester cheese that is pushed down the hill, given a one-second head start, and then chased by dozens of competitors.

Cooper's Hill is very steep, and in some places the slope is almost vertical.

It's very difficult for racers to stay on their feet! Often, they tumble downhill.

BEWARE OF FLYING CHEESE

The first person to get to the bottom of the hill wins the cheese! In 2013, the real cheese was replaced with a foam version for the safety of racers and spectators alike. The cheese can reach up to 70 mph (113 kph) on its way down the hill and can cause some serious damage!

Gloucester cheese has been made in Gloucestershire for more than 500 years.

A CHEESY HISTORY

The race is a local tradition that is believed to be at least 600 years old and may originate from a pagan ceremony celebrating the beginning of the new year. But 600 years is a drop in the bucket of our long relationship with cheese! Traces of milk proteins found in ceramic strainers in what is today Poland show that people were heating and straining milk to make cheese more than 7,500 years ago.

The holes you sometimes see in cheeses are called "eyes." They are the result of gases produced by friendly bacteria during the aging process.

The risk of injury doesn't deter people from chasing their dream of being a cheese-rolling champion!

Contests in Mythology

Mythology from around the world features gods, goddesses, spirits, and magical beings competing with one another. The world of myth isn't so different from our own world, except that the contests in legends often involve magic, seemingly impossible tasks, or truly monumental feats of strength.

POETRY SLAM

Norse mythology from Scandinavia tells the story of a poetry battle between the gods Thor and Odin. Thor, returning from an adventure, meets a ferryman named Harbard, who is Odin in disguise. Odin refuses to carry Thor across a fjord on his boat. The two gods battle in verse, bragging about their heroic deeds and insulting each other—with poetry!

YOU'RE GOING DOWN

The legendary ball game of the ancient Olmec, Aztec, and Maya worlds, played in real life by each of these Central American cultures, also occurs in Maya myths. Humans and the lords of the underworld battled by playing this game, which involves bouncing a hard rubber ball off their legs and bodies (no hands allowed) and aiming the ball at small stone hoops. In mythology, the ball court was a portal to Xibalba, the Maya underworld.

WEAVING CONTEST

In a legend from the Yoruba people of West Africa, the water goddess Olokun challenged the creator god Olorun to a weaving contest to see which of them was the more powerful and creative. Olokun was an incredible weaver, but Olorun had a secret spy working for him: the chameleon Agemo. Agemo would hide in Olokun's weaving, changing his skin to match her colors and patterns. Then he'd run back to Olorun and the god would use that information to weave an even more elaborate and beautiful cloth.

AND MORE WEAVING...

In ancient Greek mythology, a mortal woman named Arachne was the best weaver in the world. She boasted that nobody could surpass her skill, and the goddess Athena challenged her to a weaving contest to prove it. Athena wove a gorgeous tapestry depicting mortals being struck down by the gods for boastfulness (not very subtle). Arachne wove an even more beautiful tapestry depicting scenes of gods misleading and abusing mortals (also not subtle). Athena was so angry at her defeat that she turned Arachne into a spider!

In ancient Greece, relaxing and drinking wine with friends while discussing philosophy, poetry, and the latest gossip was a common activity for men in the upper classes of society. During these parties, or *symposia*, the men were entertained by dancers and musicians, and they reclined on cushioned couches. And in the 6th and 5th centuries BCE, there was another form of entertainment— *cottabus*, or "wine-slinging."

Wine Slinging

THE ANCIENT GREEKS KNEW HOW TO PARTY

GRAPE EXPECTATIONS

In ancient Greece, wine was typically drunk out of wide, shallow cups (called *kylikes*), and it wasn't as carefully filtered as most wine is today. This meant that little bits of grape skin or other sediment were often left behind at the bottom of the wine cup. So why not make a game out of getting that gunk out of your cup to prepare it for your next drink?

You could try this game at home with a cup of water... though you may want to try it outside. *Cottabus* is a messy game!

WINE NOT?

There were a few different ways to play *cottabus*, but they all involved skilfully tossing the wine lees (the bottom-of-the-cup gunk) at a target. Sometimes the game involved trying to knock small brass disks off a pole, causing them to clatter to the ground. In another version the target was a set of small disks floating in a large dish of water. The object was to flick your leftover wine out of your cup so that it landed on and sank one of the disks. Though simple, this game required dexterity and skill, which a player might lose after a few cups of wine!

ANCIENT OLYMPICS

The ancient Greeks loved making up competitions so much that they invented the most famous contest the world has ever seen: the Olympics!

Worm Charming

DO YOU HAVE THE MAGIC TOUCH?

How do you charm a worm? Do you give it compliments? (*You're looking very pink today... I love that new tunnel you dug!*) Do you present it with a gift of artisanal soil? Actually, worm charming, or "worm grunting," really only requires one thing: vibrations. In this contest, people compete to see who can tempt the most worms to the surface!

> Quick! Run!

> I don't have legs!

GOOD VIBRATIONS

Worms sense the underground world around them through vibrations, and when those vibrations get too close, the worms head to the surface to avoid tunneling predators such as moles. By creating similar vibrations on the surface, contestants can trick worms into popping up aboveground. Competitors may tap the ground with sticks, poke it with forks, bang drums, shake tambourines, or even dance! Anything to fool the worms into coming to the surface.

Prodigy

One world champion, Sophie Smith, got a whopping 567 worms when she was just 10 years old!

PRAISE THE WORMS!

Worms eat decaying plant material, which helps break it down into nice, healthy soil. Their tunnels also help keep soil loose and airy, which is great for plant roots. If you want a happy garden, make sure you have earthworms!

TAKE THE BAIT

Human worm charmers aren't luring worms for a tasty snack (eww), though they might be looking for fishing bait. During worm-charming competitions, the goal is quantity. The "playing field" is divided into sections of equal size, and the person who has the most worms in their collecting bucket after an hour wins the trophy.

EARLY BIRD CATCHES THE WORM

Humans aren't the only ones to use vibrations to trick worms! Birds often tap the ground with their feet, as if dancing, when looking for tasty worms to eat. Wood turtles also stomp their feet when looking for a wormy meal.

Lumberjack Championships

WELCOME TO THE TREE-CHOPPING OLYMPICS

Lumberjacks, who cut down trees for use in various industries, have challenging and dangerous jobs. They have to be able to do a lot of difficult tasks in order to turn a tall tree into logs and boards that can be used for building. So when lumberjacks get very, very good at these skills... they show them off!

TIMBER!

The Lumberjack World Championships began in 1960 in the city of Hayward, Wisconsin, and are held there every year. There are events for both men and women, with each event showcasing a specific skill. Some of the events include speed-sawing, log-chopping, and logrolling—which involves two contestants on top of a log that is floating in water. Each contestant must try to spin the log with their feet to knock their opponent into the water while trying to keep their own footing!

Another popular event is the speed climb. Contestants must race up and back down a cedar pole, 90 ft (27 m) tall, using climbing shoes and a special climbing strap. The world record for this event was set in 2006 by Brian Bartow, who got all the way up and down the pole in just 19.87 seconds!

Expert tree climbers use special metal spikes on the soles of their boots to help them grip tree trunks.

During the 19th and early 20th centuries, massive logs would often be floated down rivers, steered by lumberjacks standing on top of them! This inspired the logrolling event.

The double buck is performed by a team of two who push and pull their saw as fast as they can to cut a slice from a log.

Axe throwing wasn't part of a traditional lumberjack's skills, but it sure is fun!

EVENT EXPLANATIONS

Hot saw: chainsawing

Single/double buck: an individual/duo slices a log with a saw

Jack and Jill: male-female pairs chop at standing poles with axes, trying to be the first to bring theirs crashing down

Jill and Jill: a two-woman team tries to be the fastest to chop down a standing pole

Underhand chop: a single competitor tries to fell a standing pole with an underhanded swing

Standing block chop: competitors try to split thick chunks of wood with as few axe blows as possible

Springboard chop: competitors try to chop through a vertical log… while standing on a springboard attached to the log several feet off the ground!

Boom run: sprinting the length of several floating logs in a straight line

Some wood is still cut using traditional methods, but chainsaws and machinery are often preferred these days.

Cockroach Racing

TIME TO SHOW THESE CRITTERS SOME RESPECT

The most popular cockroach racing event originated in 1981 at a casino in Brisbane, Australia, when two locals argued about whether Brisbane's cockroaches were the fastest in Australia. It's now held every year on Australia Day (January 26), and the proceeds from the event are given to charity. Cockroaches are placed in the center of a circle marked on the ground and released. The roach that reaches the outside of the circle the fastest is the winner.

A WORLDWIDE PHENOMENON

A cockroach racing event is also held at the Carnegie Museum of Natural History in Pennsylvania. The insect "athletes" have goofy names and profiles on the museum's website. Contenders include Franklin "Supersonic" Carnegie, who (according to his profile) enjoys white-water rafting and sushi, and Cupcake "Speedy" Carnegie, who loves fudge brownies and painting. The roaches use their sensitive antennae to feel their way around the course!

Cockroach racing is usually held inside a circular course. It's tough to teach roaches how to follow a track...

AMAZING ROACHES

Cockroaches can zip along at around 3 mph (5 kph). If they were human-sized, they would run at 200 mph (322 kph)!

Cockroaches can "hear" by feeling vibrations around them using sensitive hairs on their legs.

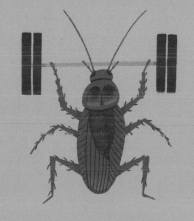

Roaches are incredibly strong and can survive forces up to 900 times their body weight!

NOT JUST PESTS

There are thousands of species of cockroaches worldwide, though only about 30 of those species are thought of as household pests. The largest species of cockroach can grow to around 4 in (10 cm) in length! Cockroaches may be unpopular indoors, but outdoors, they are extremely useful disposers of dead plant and animal material. They help keep ecosystems healthy.

A cockroach can survive for up to a week without its head! This is because roaches breathe through tiny holes throughout their body.

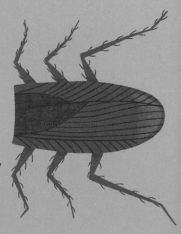

Vibes

An emotional performance is a must, so really FEEL your music!

Cool costumes are highly encouraged and contribute to a contestant's score.

Air Guitar Champs

ROCKING OUT FOR WORLD PEACE

Jazz music was once famously described by Miles Davis as being all about "the notes you don't play." But for the Air Guitar World Championships in Finland, it's rock and roll that... isn't being played. Contestants must wield their imaginary guitars for 60 seconds of fiery rock performance, showcasing their unique skills in mimicking riffs and chords, and shredding solos.

TRY TO PLAY THIS

The long, narrow part of an electric guitar is called the neck, and some electric guitars have more than one. The most necks ever attached to a single guitar is 12! The instrument was made in 2002 by the Japanese artist Yoshihiko Satoh.

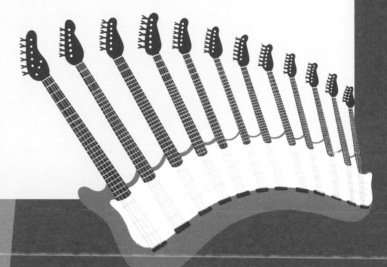

You don't **actually have to know how to play guitar to compete, but you need to look like you know what you're doing!**

GET YOUR GROOVE ON

Performers jump, dance, writhe, and work the stage in incredible costumes and with intricate routines. Some of the amazing competitor names from recent years include Airistotle, Nordic Thunder, Günther Love, Sonyk Rok, and Mr. Magnet. If you were an air guitar superstar, what would you call yourself?

WORLD PEACE

Despite the rock-and-roll attitude, the purpose of the Air Guitar World Championships is to promote world peace. According to the contest organizers, "wars would end, climate change stop, and all bad things disappear, if all the people in the world played the air guitar."

Dung Spitting

THE WORLD'S MOST CREATIVE USE FOR KUDU POOP

?!

Think of the most bizarre competition you can possibly imagine. Go on, let your imagination run wild. Really let your creativity loose. Did you come up with a competition based on spitting antelope poop? Believe it or not, this is a popular sport in South Africa, where it's called *bokdrol spoeg*.

AN ACQUIRED TASTE

The poop of choice for this contest comes from the kudu, an African antelope with majestic, spiraling horns and a delicately striped coat. Kudus, like most antelope and other types of deer, poop little pellets about the size of chocolate chips. In South Africa, competitors put (preferably old, dried-out) kudu dung in their mouths, take a deep breath, and PTOOEY! They spit the pellet as far as they can.

Kudus are very agile and can jump as far as 11 ft (3.5 m).

NASTY TRICK

Bokdrol spoeg contests are usually informal (and often involve tourists). The record is held by a man named Shaun van Rensburg, who reportedly spat a kudu pellet just over 49 ft (15 m). Part of the competition is about distance spitting, but another element is simply tricking people into putting kudu poop into their mouths. Nobody has yet asked the kudu what they think about this activity. And, just to be clear—NEVER put poop in your mouth, dear reader. Leave this to the, err, experts.

Male kudus use their massive spiral horns to wrestle with each other over females during mating season.

THIS COFFEE TASTES LIKE...

One of the most expensive coffees in the world is made from coffee cherries that have been eaten, partially digested, and pooped out by Asian palm civets. This process is said to add complexity to the aroma and taste of the roasted beans. Delicious.

Skyscraper Running

TRICKY ON SO MANY LEVELS

The Empire State Building in New York City is 1,250 ft (380 m) tall at its roof—and an antenna adds an extra 204 ft (62 m). Around four million tourists visit the building each year to take in the breathtaking views. And once every year, a small group of people gather at the ground floor to sprint their way up all 86 flights of stairs!

EPIC ENGINEERING

The Empire State Building is so tall that it had to be specially designed to withstand high winds. Its internal steel structure is an important part of its construction. It stops the building from swaying!

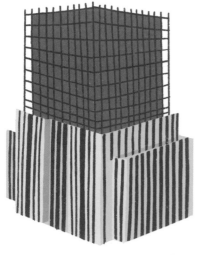

Record

When it was completed in 1931, the Empire State Building was the world's tallest building.

STAIRWAY TO EXHAUSTION

Paul Crake from Australia once got to the top in 9 minutes, 33 seconds. If you visit the Empire State Building, you can see if you can beat his time... or you can take the elevator, which will get you to the 86th floor in around a minute.

ICONIC

The Empire State Building has been featured in more than 250 TV shows and movies, the first of which was *King Kong* in 1933. The movie features a famous scene where the giant ape scales the Empire State Building, swatting off airplanes as he climbs. The building is also the focus of pop artist Andy Warhol's 1964 movie *Empire*, which is eight hours and five minutes of footage of the building.

Growing Giants

All over the world, people love to garden as a hobby, but some people take growing their fruits and vegetables to a whole new level. Growing gigantic produce can take months of hard work, but the results are spectacular. There are many different contests for growing the biggest produce. Let's take a look! Maybe you will be inspired to take up this hobby yourself...

RECORD-BREAKER

Peter Glazebrook of Nottinghamshire, England, has held multiple world records for the largest garden produce. He has grown the world's heaviest cauliflower, heaviest potato, and longest leek. Glazebrook is a legend on the giant-vegetable scene who has competed for more than 30 years!

BIG BERRIES

The Egton Bridge Old Gooseberry Society, founded all the way back in 1800, happens each year in Yorkshire, England. Gooseberries are carefully nurtured until they become gigantic. One winner grew a gooseberry the size of a golf ball. That may not sound like much, but it was 16 times heavier than an average gooseberry. For comparison, if you grew an apple that was 16 times bigger than usual, it'd be about the size of a watermelon!

PUMPKIN SPLAT

In the city of Littleton, Colorado, giant pumpkins are used to entertain crowds after the gourds have been weighed for a growing competition. Once the weights are in and a winner has been selected, the pumpkins are hoisted about 100 ft (30 m) into the air by a crane and then released to smash into the ground below.

MOOSE BREAKFAST

After the State Fair in Alaska, gardeners who have grown enormous produce usually donate their giant veggies to the Alaska Wildlife Conservation Center. Giant vegetables are amazing to look at but are usually too tough or bitter for humans to enjoy. The local wildlife, including moose, bears, and bison, love these monster veggies!

ZUCCHINI CARS

In Boulder, Colorado, giant zucchini that have already been judged for their size and weight are recycled into model "cars" for the Great Zucchini Race. Wooden wheels are stuck onto the zucchini and the veggiemobiles are raced down a ramp for glory and bragging rights.

Pumpkin Regatta

THE ULTIMATE TEST OF SPEED AND PUMPKINS

Each year, over Thanksgiving weekend (which, in Canada, happens in October), thousands of people arrive in Windsor for the annual Pumpkin Regatta! Competitors hollow out giant pumpkins to make boats. They then attempt to paddle their creations down a course, 2,625 ft (800 m) long, across Lake Pisiquid.

HENRY DAVID THOREAU

The history of giant pumpkins in North America goes back to the writer Henry David Thoreau, who grew a pumpkin in 1857 that weighed 123 lb (56 kg)! He wrote about it in a book called *Wild Fruits*, which he never finished.

CHOOSE YOUR PUMPKIN

There are three categories in which pumpkin-paddlers can compete: motor, experimental, and paddling. The motorized pumpkins typically make it across the lake in about seven or eight minutes. The paddlers take around half an hour. The experimental pumpkin crafts... well, they just do their own thing.

The very first Pumpkin Regatta had only five contestants.

IT WASN'T ALWAYS SO SILLY

The pumpkin regatta showcases giant pumpkins, but these orange gourds haven't always been big enough for boats, or even Halloween lanterns. The oldest evidence for people growing pumpkins comes from what is today Mexico, and dates to between 7,000 and 5,500 BCE! These early pumpkins were small, hard, and dense. They could be stored over the winter season when food was scarce.

TYPES OF PUMPKIN CRAFT

Motorized

Paddling

Experimental

Gurning Contest

WHO CAN MAKE THE MOST MEMORABLE FACE?

The World Gurning Championships is held every year at the Egremont Crab Fair in the United Kingdom. The crabs in question are actually crab apples—no crustaceans here. A number of events take place each year during the fair, including wheelbarrow racing and trying to climb up a greased pole. But the gurning competition is a crowd favorite!

FUNNY FACES

Gurning is an old English term for making a funny face. A typical gurn involves sticking out your lower jaw and covering your upper lip with your lower lip, and maybe crossing your eyes or sticking out your tongue for extra effect.

YE OLDE FAIRE

The fair dates all the way back to 1267 CE, when it was established by King Henry III, in the later half of the Middle Ages. That's more than 750 years ago! At the time, the fair would have been a large public market. Traveling salespeople could set up temporary shops, and locals could buy or barter for the things they needed.

HORSING AROUND

Gurning contests have been traditional in rural English towns for a long time. Usually, the contestant sticks his or her head through a horse collar and pulls their best face for the crowd. A winner is selected from each of the three categories: men, women, and children. Peter Jackman, a man who won the championships four times, had his teeth removed so he could make sillier faces! That's what you call dedication.

Go ahead and try gurning in a mirror! Do you think you could win the competition?

The Rock Riddle

A HISTORY MYSTERY THAT TOOK CENTURIES TO SOLVE

For years, a message inscribed on a rock more than 200 years ago in the French village of Plougastel-Daoulas has mystified everyone who read it. In 2019, the village offered a reward of 2,000 Euros to anyone who could figure out what the writing was meant to say. The competition was on...

SECRET CODE

On one side of the slab of rock is a jumbled mix of capital letters arranged in 20 lines. There are also pictures of a sailboat and a heart, and the dates 1786 and 1787 are carved into the rock. Most of the letters are in the standard French alphabet, but some letters are written backward, and some of the O's are written in the Scandinavian style, with a bar through them (Ø). What on earth could it all mean?

AS CLEAR AS MUD

When you look at the inscriptions, they don't make much sense as French words. In one section the letters read, "ROC AR B ... DRE AR GRIO SE EVELOH AR VIRIONES BAOAVEL." Another line says, "OBBIIE: BRISBVILAR ... FROIK ... AL". One theory is that the writing is related to naval forts that were built in this area in the late 1700s, when France and England were at war. The inscription could be a memorial.

Try to come up with your own secret code and see if any of your friends can crack it!

SOLVING THE RIDDLE

The person who carved the rock may not have been very good at writing and could have spelled out the words as they heard them. In 2020, two teams of contestants were awarded the prize money for their translations.

"He was the incarnation of courage and joie de vivre. Somewhere on the island he was struck and he is dead."

Winning entry 1

"Serge died when with no skill at rowing, his boat was tipped over by the wind."

Winning entry 2

One of the language experts who translated the riddle suggested that the writer spoke Old Breton, a dialect spoken in Brittany, the region of France where the stone was found.

Donkey Polo

THE STORY OF A DONKEY-LOVING SPORTS SUPERFAN

During the Tang Dynasty in ancient China, which lasted from 618 CE to 907 CE, anyone who was anyone played polo. In this challenging sport, players used long mallets to hit a ball from horseback, driving it toward a goal. You had to be a skilled rider to play the sport well! And in the Tang Dynasty, it wasn't just horses that were used to play...

STUDYING THE BONES

Donkeys are often used to carry things, but the ones in Cui Shi's tomb were relatively small and had markings on their bones that showed they spent a lot of time sprinting. The scientists who studied the bones think that these donkeys were probably polo mounts.

ENTER THE DONKEYS

Noblemen enjoyed polo, and those who were victorious in matches gained elevated status. But if noblewomen wanted to play, they were discouraged from the fast, dangerous, horse-powered sport. Instead, they played polo on donkeys! Donkeys are shorter, stockier, and a bit slower than their horsey cousins, and the risk of being bucked off the saddle was lower, making donkey polo a less dangerous version of the game.

RIDING INTO THE AFTERLIFE

One woman, Cui Shi, who died in 878 CE, loved donkey polo and her team of donkeys so much that she may have been buried with some of them! Cui Shi was the wife of a high-ranking general named Bao Gao, and the pair of them were written about in burial inscriptions and historical documents as polo champions. The donkeys buried with Cui Shi may have been some of her favorite mounts.

Kite Fighting

A FIGHT WITH STRINGS ATTACHED

Kite flying is a popular pastime in several countries, including Afghanistan in the Middle East. But this isn't just a case of sending a kite up to dance in the breeze— it means fighting! The objective is to skilfully pilot your kite to snap another flyer's string.

LET'S GO FLY A KITE

The string used in kite fighting is specially made of strong twine coated with glue and finely crushed glass, which turns the string into a blade when it's pulled taut. Kite fighters compete in teams of two. One person holds the spool of kite string, and the other maneuvers the kite by skillfully twitching the string.

READY FOR THE WEEKEND

Most kite fights happen on Fridays. Kite flyers head for rooftops and hillsides, carrying stacks of kites to compete with. Often, flyers will go through several kites in a single day, which is why the kites are made from relatively cheap materials.

KITE RUNNING

Afghan kites are usually made of bamboo frames and tissue paper by local artisans whose craft is often passed down through a single family for generations. When two kites fight and one's string is snapped, then the kite running begins. Children sprint after the defeated kites as they drift to the ground, chasing them until they can retrieve them. This is often a way for children who can't afford kites to fly one of their own.

The skies over Afghan cities are often filled with brightly colored kites swooping through the air.

Eating Contests

Eating is something to be enjoyed and savored, usually in the presence of friends and family. At least, that's normally what happens. However, some people decided that eating was a perfect opportunity for more competitions! Usually, people compete to eat the most of a single type of food, or to eat food the fastest—or sometimes both!

HOT STUFF

Hunan province, China, is famous for its spicy cuisine. At the annual Hunan chilli pepper festival, competitors line up to see who can chomp down the most fresh chillis in the shortest amount of time. Leave this one to the extreme spice-seekers... too many hot peppers can give you a serious tummy ache!

AMERICAN EATERS

Eating competitions are so popular in the United States that there is an organization that oversees professional contests across the nation. A legend of professional competitive eating is Joey Chestnut. Joey has held more than 50 world records for eating hot dogs, chicken wings, tacos, gyoza, and more. Meanwhile, Raina Huang, a competitive eater and social media star, faced off against two giant rabbits and defeated them in a salad-eating contest!

FROM FARM TO TABLE

A 17th-century English farmer named Nicholas Wood, given the nickname The Great Eater of Kent, might be one of the earliest examples of a professional competitive nosher. Wood became famous for his appetite. At one notable dinner, he ate 60 eggs, a leg of lamb, and a handful of pies!

Glossary

Ammunition
Objects like bullets, arrows, or cannonballs that are loaded into, and then fired from, weapons.

Archaeologist
A person who learns about the lives of people in the past by studying the materials those people left behind.

Areca nut tree
A species of palm tree that grows in the Pacific region, Asia, and parts of eastern Africa.

Aztecs
An ancient Mesoamerican culture known for its art, architecture, and writing. The Aztec empire occupied what is today central Mexico from 1300 CE to 1521 CE, around 700–500 years ago.

Bearding
A behavior seen in bees that involves clustering on the outside of a hive, looking kind of like a beard. This helps the bee larvae (baby bees) in the hive to stay cool on hot days.

Bedouin
A nomadic group of people from the deserts of the Arabian Peninsula and surrounding areas.

Bog mummies
Human remains that have been extremely well preserved in peat bogs.

Calligraphy
Artistic writing, usually done with ink and a brush or pen.

Carbon dioxide
A gas that is produced naturally by organisms who breathe in oxygen. It is also produced by things that burn gas or oil, like cars. Too much carbon dioxide in the air is harmful for the planet.

Clan (Scottish)
A group of closely related families that often live close by one another.

Colonial empire
A political power or country that has used military and oppressive force to take over and rule other places.

Cottabus
An ancient Greek game in which players try to fling the last drops of wine from their cups to knock a brass plate down from a pole.

Decibel
A unit of measurement that indicates how loud a sound is.

Dragon boat
A long, oar-powered boat, originating from southern China, with a carved dragon's head on the front.

Ecosystem

A community of living things (organisms) that interact with one another in an environment.

Gurning

Making a silly face.

Hibernation

A state of heavy sleep entered by many types of animals during winter months (or other times of the year when conditions are tough).

Larvae

A baby insect.

Lumberjack

A person who cuts down trees for wood.

Lunar calendar

A system of tracking days of the year based on the phases of the moon.

Maya

An ancient Mesoamerican (modern-day Mexico) culture known for its art, writing, architecture, mathematics, and calendar system. The Maya are not extinct—there are descendant communities living today.

Mesopotamia

A region of western Asia between the Tigris and Euphrates rivers. Today, this region is occupied by Iraq, although historically, the Mesopotamian culture included parts of modern-day Iran, Kuwait, Syria, and Turkey.

Olmecs

An ancient group of people that lived in what is today Veracruz and Tabasco, Mexico, between 1600 BCE and 400 BCE (around 3,600 years ago to 2,400 years ago).

Pagan

A term for a person who holds religious beliefs other than those of the primary world religions.

Patent

A legal document certifying that a person has the right to be the sole maker, user, or seller of an invention.

Peat

Spongy layers of partially decomposed vegetation, saturated in water, in wetlands like swamps, bogs, and moors.

Persia

The historical name of the region of southwestern Asia occupied by modern Iran.

Primates

A group of related species that includes monkeys, apes, humans, and lemurs.

Sumo wrestler

An athlete who competes in the traditional Japanese form of wrestling known as sumo.

Zaraniq tribe

A group of people who traditionally live in the Tihama-al-Yemen, a desert plain next to the Red Sea.

Index

This has been a
NEON SQUID
production

To mom and dad, for being superlative parents and filling my childhood with books; to Naomi, for being the best partner and supporter.

Author: Anna Goldfield
Illustrator: Hannah Riordan

Editorial Assistant: Malu Rocha
US Editor: Allison Singer Kushnir
Proofreader: Laura Gilbert
Indexer: Elizabeth Wise

Copyright © 2023 St. Martin's Press
120 Broadway, New York, NY 10271

Created for St. Martin's Press by Neon Squid
The Stables, 4 Crinan Street, London, N1 9XW

EU representative: Macmillan Publishers Ireland Ltd, 1st Floor, The Liffey Trust Centre, 117–126 Sheriff Street Upper, Dublin 1, D01 YC43

10 9 8 7 6 5 4 3 2 1

Library of Congress Cataloging-in-Publication Data is available.

Printed and bound by Vivar Printing in Malaysia.

ISBN: 978-1-684-49286-2

Published in April 2023.

www.neonsquidbooks.com